AWay with Words: The Voice of Silence

by
Erin Wiley

Copyright © 2022, Erin Wiley

All rights reserved. No part of this book may be used or reproduced by any means, graphic, electronic, or mechanical, including photocopying, recording, taping or by any information storage retrieval system without the written permission of the publisher except in the case of brief quotations embodied in critical articles and reviews.

WWW.ERINWILEYWRITES.COM

AWay with Words: The Voice of Silence

ISBN: 979-8-9870496-0-0

Edited and formatted by
Water2WinePress Publishing House,
a Subsidiary of Ink Well Spoken
www.inkwellspoken.com

Cover Design by Liberated Living, LLC

WATER2WINEPRESS
PUBLISHING HOUSE

*This book is dedicated to those who Seek.
May your "finding" times be short-lived,
chased ever joyfully by the next reentry into the
beautiful unfolding of Life's mystery.
Journey on...*

HAIKU

When the Silence joins
The Voice, Truth can lift its song:
Harmony, Peace, Love

CONTENTS

PREFACE	**p. ix**
ACKNOWLEDGEMENTS	**p. xiii**
INTRODUCTION	**p. 1**
PART ONE: "Yes, Lord!"	**p. 3**
Freefall	p. 6
All This Gray	p. 8
Telepathy	p. 10
The Truth	p. 13
The Art of S-E-R-V-I-C-E*	p. 19
Reflected	p. 22
Butterflew*	p. 29
Toxic	p. 35
Yeah, Write	p. 39
Maternal Sense*	p. 45
Speak	p. 48
Eulogize Me	p. 50
"Yes, Lord!" Conclusion	**p. 55**
PART TWO: "Soar"	**p. 57**
Raindrop Song	p. 60
Wake Up	p. 62
Meet Connie*	p. 67
I, AManda*	p. 73
Move!*	p. 75
Intolerance 9-1-1	p. 78

Tell My Daughter	p. 82
Color Blind	p. 86
And Love Held the World*	p. 93
Numb*	p. 99
The Creed*	p. 105
"Soar" Conclusion	**p. 110**

EPILOGUE   **p. 112**
Cloudy Wonder	p. 114
"Cloud E Wonder" by Jackie W.	p. 117

ABOUT THE AUTHOR   **p. 119**

* indicates that some additional commentary precedes or follows the piece

PREFACE

*F*or as long as I can remember, I have loved numbers. I love to calculate, analyze, and solve and that has always been true. It serves me professionally and casually, and is a very visible attribute that I'm known for. But interestingly, (and on a lesser-known level), I've also always loved words... perhaps even more. I love to read, I love to write, and I love to talk and listen. There's just so much to be gained from each carefully (or haphazardly) crafted arrangement of characters or sounds, no matter the language. It brings me true joy to play around with words and see what kinds of cool things I can express. To me, writing is like hosting a party on a page and watching how all of the words show up and play together. So much fun!

When I look back, the enthusiasm and enjoyment I receive from wordsmithing has always been there; I just didn't actively acknowledge it. Despite countless compliments and expressions of appreciation for my writing skills, I somehow remained somewhat distant from this aspect of myself. It was almost like I knew it was true - I just didn't really need to pay any attention to it. I can't say whether it was because I was so accustomed to my own written voice, or if I'd subconsciously screened myself out of the possibility that I could have a gift - something special and unique - that could set me apart. There's a whole 'nother book that could be written about my discomfort with my own "shine," but I won't go there now! Suffice it to say, if not for the kind words, generous compliments, and truly heartfelt encouragement from various people over the years, you would not be reading this today.

For years, people have insisted that I write a book. And for years, I've always given lip-service to being open to the idea, but without having any real expectation that I would follow through. I couldn't see a clear and concrete vision of what "the book" would be, so it stayed on my mental shelf, collecting dust unless someone brought it up again. Any words, insights, or declarations I needed to make went into my private vault and stayed there, silent and hidden away. And I'm grateful for that. I understand now that I needed to come to an awareness and acceptance of my own voice.

Subjecting myself to the scrutiny and input of others prematurely would have left me obsessively watching for external validation and approval, likely stunting my own expression if I didn't receive it as I'd hoped. In that silent space, there was only me, my truth, and the Divine Source that gifted it to me. In such company, I discovered my authentic Voice.

While discovering that voice was the first step, being willing to lift it beyond my comfortable spaces was a completely different matter... until spoken word entered my life. That entry happened in a hilariously unexpected way - which is one of my life's greatest and fondest memories. Suffice it to say, I formed a friendship with an incredible mentor who encouraged me, without reservation, to get on stage at an open mic event. I'm generally at ease with standing up and talking to a room full of people about any given topic of interest. Performing my own written work in front of an audience was a completely different scenario, but I quickly learned that the spoken word environment was one of openness and respect. The blend of both seasoned and brand-new artists coalesced into a community where every unique perspective was unconditionally welcomed and appreciated... including mine! My authentic Voice was loosed once I realized its potential for power, when unfiltered and unapologetic. Whenever I stepped on stage, I experienced the exhilaration of true freedom of expression without the need for acceptance.

What lies before you is the fruit of my journey: the words and insights that were revealed in the Silence, then entrusted to my Voice. While I believe poetry is best left fully to the interpretation of the reader, throughout this book I have provided some words of reflection in order to invite you deeper into my own experience. In those moments, while I will share my thoughts, I leave you with the important task of finding your own insights and revelations. As *"beauty is in the eye of the beholder,"* wisdom is in the ear of the listener, and I invoke the Silence as translator, interpreter, whisperer, and guide for your passage through these pages.

ACKNOWLEDGEMENTS

I always enjoy reading the acknowledgements section of the books I pick up. Getting a small glimpse of the story behind the story, and those who supported and made way for the author to write it, is a real treat. So, it is my honor to lavish praise all over my amazing circle of love!

First and foremost, to my husband and most devoted fan, Charles: you believed in and affirmed my Voice long before I even realized it was there. Your unique brand of "encouragement" and support is an essential part of my daily life and this journey to Becoming the woman you already see. Thank you, my love, for keeping life intriguing!

To my incredible daughters, Naira and Sienna: you have inherited your father's ability to see and love me in a way that inspires and encourages me to soar. You gift me with sincere Hope for the best each day, and the Grace to see and do all things with love. I see in each of you, a powerful force for good, for love, for change, and for peace in a world that desperately needs you, but probably isn't ready to handle you... yet. Thank you for choosing me to be your mom in this lifetime so I can watch you shine your light and guide us safely through the dark places. I love you!

To the daughter of my heart, CFW: you may never read this or even know that it exists, but you have been one of my most powerful instructors about healing through writing. You are the song of Faith that my soul is constantly singing and I love you as my own.

To my parents Dave and Greta, and my brother Damon: for the gift of a childhood overflowing with love, support, and acceptance... and the treasure of an adulthood with an abundance of the same. We share a love for the written word that I recognize as the anchor of any gift I have in that arena. Though we each gravitate toward different genres, it is your sincere appreciation for an author's unique style and voice that has empowered me to find my own. Rather than the typical "wind beneath my wings" sentiment, I consider you the Love Force infused into the space between each line I write, and I hope you find yourselves and my love for you there.

To the rest of my village: you may not recognize me in some of these words... or perhaps my true Self has spoken louder than I realized over the years and I'm the one who didn't hear Her! Whatever the case may be, you have each poured into me in your own way throughout this journey, and I'm grateful.

To Eric "E-Baby" Smith: I don't know anyone else who could say their bachelorette party was the catalyst to writing a (non-scandalous) book, but here we are! Your willingness to generously share your talent, your time, your wisdom, and your support is the mark of a true mentor. I am grateful to count myself among those who have blossomed under your care and can also call you friend.

To Kyle Alexander, gentle bully and coach extraordinaire: for pushing me, guiding me, and challenging me to "own my shine" without losing who I am along the way. Thank you for constantly reminding me that this is still only the beginning, and for seeing and championing the possibilities that lie ahead. Let's go Grounds Crew!

To the spiritual teachers who have opened doorways to the Divine for me through personal interaction, or by sharing your wisdom widely enough that it reached me from afar - I am eternally grateful. Leah G. Johnson, Monsignor

Raymond East, Gerald Hopeck, Pastor Greg Stamper and Pastor Yolanda Batts, Reverend Michael Bernard Beckwith, Dianne Stewart-Hamlin, Mirabai Starr, Father Richard Rohr, and more: each of you has freely shared and consistently demonstrated how your personal connection to the Divine fuels and fires every aspect of your life… which then allows you to give the best of yourself to the world. Thank you for lighting the way!

To Emma Sembly-Brodie of "Just Folks: Conversations with Emma" (YouTube) for your sacred "Yes", which finally turned the key to unlock my own. And to dear Marjorie Schenk, whose simple enjoyment and appreciation of my work has shown me that only good can come from freely sharing my true Self with others. The friendship shared by the two of you is truly Divine!

To Reggie and Quiana Kee of Water2Wine Publishing House: for your easygoing but matter-of-fact way of seeing my vision with certainty, even while I was still dealing in the realm of possibility. Your uncomplicated confidence in the worth of this work, before you ever read a single word, grounded me in a way I didn't know I needed. Thank you for your guidance and friendship.

To the wonderfully talented Jackie W.: thank you for taking the self-image I've carried in my heart and giving Her a form that I can finally SEE...and share. I can't wait to see where your gifts take you from here!

And finally, to you, kind soul who has found your way to this book and is willing to see what lies ahead... my deepest gratitude: I am certain that you hold this in your hands because your soul is among those that called it forth. I am honored that I have the privilege of contributing in some way to your journey. Please know that, in your reading of this work, you have become a living affirmation of my own pathway to Becoming.

Thank you for accompanying me, here at the beginning...

INTRODUCTION

*H*ow do you write the introduction to a book you don't feel responsible for creating? It feels pretty disingenuous to say that I'm fit to give some form of summary or preview of what's to come in the pages ahead. Quite frankly, I don't consider it my business to tell you what to expect. I suppose that's equal parts surrender to whatever will be, and the oh-so-familiar fear that what you read might not measure up to your expectations. Whichever side of that coin I'm on today, I trust with complete conviction that your journey here will be as it should.

What I **can** say is that this collection represents my own quest to find a pathway to peace with the "in-between" spaces in my life. The most persistent of these has been my consistent vacillating between the call to use my voice to speak my truth, and the growing need to spend time in silence and contemplation. Striking a balance between these seemingly polarized positions is something that has always been challenging because, depending on the moment, it often feels like one or the other is the hungriest need, and therefore must be fed most urgently.

In these words, I have revealed to myself the answer to this near-constant conundrum. My voice is clearest when I let the Silence be my guide in using it. At the same time, my time in silence is richer, more whole, more intentional, and more sincere when I am lifting my Voice to speak my truth freely in my daily living. It is not the balance between these that I seek, but a complete and harmonious joining from which the song of my soul can emerge.

When I do away with words, I have a way with words. It is the Silence that wields the pen.

And so it is.

PART ONE: "Yes, Lord!"

My journey as a writer began in quiet, subtle ways that speak much louder to me now than they did over 10 years ago. My younger cousin (who is also one of my role models) gave me a journal for Christmas, with a liturgical dancer and the words, "Yes, Lord!" on the front cover. In it, she wrote a personal inscription where she said the cover reminded her of my "persistent and radical faith." Looking back at it now, I find it interesting that she saw my faith as "radical" at that time. While it was indeed persistent, in my eyes that was tied very much to the safe, familiar, and foundational roots of my faith tradition, which I was deeply devoted to at that time. I knew the course well, honored and testified to it with vigor, and believed that it was certainly the path for me since I was perceived to demonstrate it well and in a manner that was of service to others. I relied on obedience to direct me and, because there were good fruits from those choices, it seemed clear that my purpose was to continue in that way.

I'm grateful that something in my cousin spoke a breakaway from safety into my spirit, calling forth a stifled portion of myself to step into liberation.

The scripture on the first blank page read:

"Pleasant words are as an honeycomb, sweet to the soul, and health to the bones."
- Proverbs 16:24

In the words captured on the pages that followed, my soul's journey to that sweet freedom began.

Freefall

Ah, there it is.
The mountain I knew would come, and yet I
never expected it to actually arrive.
Yeah, I trust, but that elusive belief is always
a step behind.
So now, here I stand, befuddled, though I
shouldn't be.
Afraid, because humanity says I oughta be.
Hopeful, because somebody told me to be.
Here…because God created me to be.

Drawing from stores of courage that I never
knew I had, I take the first step.
Another and another, finding handholds and
footholds where I could swear they
weren't before.
A pull from above, a push from below…
and sometimes a push from above and
a pull from below.
This trek seems never ending, always bending,
my prayers I'm desperately sending…
and look, I'm still contending.

Before me, I see it…
the peak is waiting just ahead.
His promise is kept and I'm both ashamed for
the doubt and elated because, despite all that…
there's my ticket out.
I rise and rise and long to see that victory I
know is waiting for me!

So close now, I can almost taste it...
just one... more... step.

And there is nothing here but... me.
I turn in a circle, because surely
there must be more.
But the mirror says, "You aren't the you
that you were before."

I take a step back to consider the view.
I think I've shed some dead weight
during the climb
And maybe I look a little exhausted,
but not worn down.
I still can't see the big deal.
Until I meet the eyes of my reflection,
my image and likeness.
There I find the answers I've searched
for all along.

I see the truth of who I have always been
and who I have become.
The light reveals that what I've longed for was
right back where I started, hidden in darkness.
And, at last, I see the way.

So... I leap.

All This Gray

*So, things are supposed to be
black and white, right?
Maybe my apparent indecisiveness is not just a
personality trait, but a lifestyle.
Everywhere I turn, I'm asked: yes or no, right
or wrong, him or her, and my brain
screams in frustration.
Because they tell me it must be black or white,
and my eyes only see all this gray.*

*That glass half-empty or half-full messes with
my mind because in my mathematical world,
a half is a half is a half and why must I be
expected to choose, and therefore labeled
optimist or
pessimist, when in my eyes I'm just a realist
because they ARE the same.*

*Oh, and you want me to be a strong Black
woman, unashamed of my outer self and
focused on my inner beauty.
And yet I have to be lectured that my life must
be too stressful and I'm just "too young" to have
all this gray in my hair, because I feel no need to
dye it or cover it up.*

*Never mind that it's simply a trait that I
inherited from my daddy, I proudly own it
right along with the lessons he taught me,
which sculpted me to not give a damn about
how you might think "all this gray" looks.*

*I love the Word of God, but when I read it, then
hear it preached or see it supposedly lived, it's
like the black of the print mixed with the white
pages and made all this gray.
Because I love my Christ...
and I love my neighbor as myself,
even my neighbor that <u>doesn't</u> love Christ for
himself, and I can't understand how the way,
the truth, and the life became,
"Do things our <u>way</u>, or in <u>truth</u>,
we will ridicule and discredit your whole <u>life</u>."
I could have been Pro-Life, but if white is the
purity of life, then maybe it's the black shame,
guilt, and slander hurled to "defend" it that
creates all this gray.*

*So, forgive me if I don't automatically see things
your way... but I'm still 20/20 so it's very clear
to me. You can keep your convictions and show
the world what's black and what's white.
I'll keep some perspective and my peace, and
rest comfortably amidst all this gray.*

Telepathy

*Oooh, if you only knew what goes on
inside my head!
Oh, they aren't the raunchy thoughts,
or the silly thoughts,
or the thoughts you find it so easy to relate to.*

*The Food Network taught me that,
even if a dish looks a little scary on the inside,
with the right presentation,
you can get almost anyone to eat it up.
So, the thoughts I so easily share to make you
smile or laugh or feel comfortable?
That's all part of my... presentation.
It makes me easier to stomach.*

*But if you only knew what goes on
inside my head...
Would you be able to grasp that this
presentation was borne from an undetectable
fear of being found unacceptable?
That the smiles and laughter I display so easily
are not solely due to a healthy sense of humor
and a fun-loving nature,
but are in truth also symptoms of a need
I've been silently nursing since childhood?*

A need to be considered so safe

*and unthreatening that it would be almost
impossible NOT to like me.
A need buried so deep,
it has taken me until now to bring it
to light and see it for what it is.*

*If you could read my mind,
would the script be jagged from the battle my
inner being constantly fights against my drive
to be everything to everybody,
desperately searching for a chance to be
something... anything... to myself?*

*Perhaps my mind would whisper to you in
a sultry tone, giving voice to a sensuality
that has struggled to break free from bonds
placed by religion and society,
both of which would label me sinner or slut,
but would back away defensively were I
to blame them for my inability to distinguish
between modesty and shame.*

*Would you call me a prude because I am
somehow stimulated, but disgusted;
liberated, but uncomfortable;
passionate, but unsure of how to show it,
sometimes even in my own bed?*

Or can you see that my unwillingness to engage

*in "grown folk" talk isn't because I think I'm
better than you or am judging you,
but because I'm still seeking permission
from myself to learn how to truly let go?*

*With a glimpse into my mind,
would you watch as the child that I was,
the woman that I am,
and the creation I am destined to be struggle
to accept each other so that there
can be peace within?*

*When the child in me cries,
will you complain that she needs to toughen up?
If the woman falters,
will you shake your head in pity and disgust
because she can't seem to get it together?
When the creation emerges,
will you whisper about her past and mock her
vision of the future?
Or in her story, will you find hope
because maybe you aren't alone
in this world after all?*

*Oh, if you only knew what goes on
inside my head...
Maybe you would find the courage
to face what goes on inside of yours.*

The Truth

I have a history that you wouldn't expect.
I'm a pathological liar.
Oh, but not in the way you would think.

I don't lie to get over or get by,
but I adjust so I don't hurt or offend.
I want to bring joy and peace,
I want to uplift and encourage,
I want to make people smile and laugh...
*because it makes **me** feel good.*
And I would rather speak words that feel just as
good going out as they would coming in,
so I limit myself to that feel good language.

*But the prophets said the Word would **burst***
from their lips unwanted...
or else it would seethe and fester,
burning their insides with
each refusal to let it out,
until they found themselves
desperate to speak!

Chained to this burden of Truth
that they would rather shoulder alone
than ask someone else to carry.

I find myself tangled up in the vocal cords

*responsible for this bondage
that makes me a slave
to the very wisdom I pray for everyday!*

*I told the Mist in the Morning
about my enslaved voice and she simply
said that the Truth would set me free.*

*"You can't handle the truth,"
Jack Nicholson said,
but right now the truth
is handling ME and,
of the two of us, I'm the only one
with the means to turn the key.
And set us free... to face the truth about me.*

*The truth is that I need your love
more than I've needed my own,
which is how I got to be this way
in the first place.*

*The truth is that it's easier for me
to believe you're a liar just like me,
than to accept your compliments as truth.*

*The truth is that I'd rather see this voice as a
simple talent to dabble with because it's fun,
than a gift given to me so that I might use it to
touch lives, to reach hearts, to change the world.*

*The truth is that I would wrap myself up in
a comfortable box with my journal, my pen,
and an occasional mic if you didn't draw
me out and push me to do more.*

*Because you believe in me much more than
I believe in myself and so,
the truth is that you've given my gift the wings...
but I'm still struggling to fly.*

*But my daddy will tell you if I'm nothing else,
I'm stubborn as hell,
and so I won't stay grounded much longer.
Down here, I'm stuck in these friendly
falsehoods and loving lies,
but I know that it's time to get high.
Because the truth is... my destination is the sky.*

A Word on...
The Art of S-E-R-V-I-C-E

A couple of years into my writing journey, a dear friend of mine co-created a community space for artists and art lovers to come together for the purpose of experiencing and appreciating art in various forms. At each gathering, two or three artists would share some of their creative work, and then those gathered would engage in discussion and reflection, or could pose questions to the artists about their work.

When my friend (who later became my coach and was instrumental in the process for creating the book you're reading right now) approached me and invited me to come to the gathering as an artist, I was pretty intimidated, but willing. I was still working to accept the title of being an "artist," but I felt the space was safe enough to give it a try. I don't recall now, but I think it may have been the first time I had written a piece based on a theme provided to me by someone else. I would later discover that type of arrangement to be something I truly enjoy.

My time at the gathering provided both an opportunity for me to say more about what the words meant to me, and the privilege of hearing how it was received and interpreted by others. It was equal parts gift and validation, both of which I cherish to this day, and that experience contributed to my vision for this book.

The theme for that night was *The Art of S-E-R-V-I-C-E* and it inspired the following piece by the same name, which I fondly subtitled as, "an acrostic abounding with alliteration."

The Art of S-E-R-V-I-C-E

***S**till so surprised that this self-absorbed sista is satisfactory for the service of sending souls to the source of my salvation. I stand to spill sentences, somewhat skeptical of my own sufficiency... so I step to the side and seek to be surrendered to the Spirit who will speak in my stead. And suddenly, I'm a study of sure success, secure in my sense of status, because I'm saturated in the security of His saving grace.*

***E**very day, every emotion I experience is eligible to be expressed on the end of my pen. But I examine each, exploring for those essential elements... that it edify as it enters the ear, that it educate about the Eternal one, and that it endeavor to encourage everyone to evaluate their existence on this earth.*

***R**eally, I'd rather reserve my recitations for rambling and random rhetoric. But in Romans, it says that my reading can reveal the righteousness of God, regardless of religion. For that reason, I reflect on my revelations and I reach for the remembrances that resonate with rightness. It rescues my heart from racing and realigns it with the rhythm of my Redeemer.*

Recovered from my ridiculous repertoire of rationalizations, I realize that redemption requires that I regularly recalculate my route. That I rethink relying on reason and rediscover the road that reveals responsibilities I'd rather resist and reject, but that result in returning me to a place of rest.

Vividly, *we can voice the victories we've won over a variety of vices and villainy, voraciously feeding the vitality of that version of ourselves that will vigorously verify His power and authority with volume. Oh, but the vocalization of our vulnerabilities, or the velvety lure of our vanity, or the violence coursing through our veins... very seldom do we value the voicing of our victimization, refusing its penetration, as if its validity is voided by its violation of our virginal testimonies. But in His vision, it just verifies me as a valuable vessel.*

I've *invested infinite hours of idle time inquiring about how to increase my intimacy with God. I interrogate myself about isolated instances where I invited Him to interact with me, but I find them inadequate. Interestingly, my investigation fails to include my intercession on behalf of individuals I know and I instinctively insist that my involvement with the youth is* *more about my ineptitude than inspiration. Insightful, isn't it? I'm itching for enough intelligence to ignore my own incomplete ideas about my identity in Christ and to instead imagine my image through His impossibly, infatuated eyes.*

Can't always comprehend how clasping a hand, or chatting with a child, or consoling a companion can be called "church." But Christ calls us to care. And He cherishes every soul that comes to Him, caused by our compassion. Complications are created when I convince myself that the criteria are comprised of concepts more complex than character, charity, and concern for fellow man. I challenge you to have courage, champion His causes, and carry <u>your</u> cross.

Epilogue: I, Erin, engaged in this exercise, not to entertain or even to educate. But because this environment and its evangelistic energy excites me. Eventually, I expect that this experience, shared equally, will evolve into an electrifying example of how effortlessly, how excellently, God can use each of us to change the world. Even me.

Reflected

*I was compelled, told, encouraged,
ordered really, to pick up my pen tonight.
So, I fully expect that the words
I speak will be the words you seek.
Not because I can read your mind...
but because I insist on going
deeper and deeper into mine.
And each time I dig,
the golden glow of wisdom
and understanding shines with
a radiance that illuminates
the shadowy corners and burns away
the frozen-over pockets of my psyche
that I've kept from myself, from you,
and tried to keep from Him...*

*Because I never meant to have to unveil myself,
stripped naked and paraded
in front of strangers on a stage
with a microphone and bright lights
and a captive audience.
At no point in my existence
would I have felt that it was
your business to know
the desperate chokehold I've kept on
myself in order to maintain what
I thought was my sanity.*

*What right do you have to see me for
who I really am and to listen
to my secrets and be given
the opportunity to scoff and laugh
and ridicule me, because you can't relate
or you just don't give a damn?
Who died and made you God?*

*Oh, I see. I did.
When I chose to bury myself
under a coat of tolerance
and pacifistic tendencies,
or when I painted on the face of a clown,
but refused to include the tears,
or when I played the "I'm too strong
to ever be broken," role,
I died...I **died** and made YOU my God,
because I'd rather be able to look
you in the face with a smile than look straight
into the tormented eyes of my
own reflection and have to see... me.*

*Funny thing is, this smile, this easy laugh,
really is me... I truly enjoy
and find amusement in the life
I live every single day.
But the more I ignored or denied
the darker parts of me,
the harder it became to make*

the amusement last.
You see, no one really told me that
God is good all the time,
when they were busy telling me
I was wrong and bad and sinning.
They made it sound like God
would show up and bless me when I was good,
but that He might just send a postcard
if I was bad. The difference between
"God loves you!" and "God loves you..."
will forever be the nightmarish possibilities
I can fill in to follow the word "...but"
that they didn't say, but left hanging in the air.

My freedom came when
I stopped listening to others explain
why God loved me and started
to hear Him simply tell me for Himself.
When I examined my deep
and undetectable insecurities
and brought them to the light,
I found that it was more liberating
to name them and claim them
than to bury them or hide them
from the world in shame.
And I watched God continue
to bless me just as much
in my newly discovered brokenness,

as He had in my fabricated neat and tidiness.
And despite every insult
I've hurled at Him in anger,
every time I've vehemently
denied His existence,
or every victory I've taken sole credit for...
though I could never tell you
how I made it happen,
I still see Him smile and show me
love every single day.

I picked up my pen to write this,
not for me and not even for Him,
but for you.
Because I died and made you God...
so that when I look you in the eyes and smile,
I'll see Him looking back at me.
And maybe, just maybe... you will, too.

A Word on...
Butterflew

As an adult, I've always had a great love for the idea, the concept, the philosophy of the butterfly's experience. This cool realization that a living being could go from one form that is in itself, a whole, complete, and seemingly finished product... and then experience an overwhelming transformation into something new. That both a caterpillar and a butterfly are considered as separate entities, even though one must <u>always</u> begin as the other. It would be fascinating to know what the mindset or understanding of the caterpillar would be before its metamorphosis. Does a caterpillar know what will happen when it enters the cocoon? Once it completes the transformation, does the butterfly remember that it used to be a caterpillar and what that was like? The awe-inspiring genius found in nature provides such wonderful mysteries to muse about, and all of Creation is a feast for the imagination... including us.

Butterflew

Someone saw fit to create me.
They poured all of the components
necessary into this little sphere,
where they jumbled together
in an incoherent, formless, vast...
somethingness.
And I asked, "Is this it?"

I didn't know what "it" was,
but there was this sense that "it" was coming!
Somehow, in the midst
of the tumultuous makeup,
there was a definitive time and place
for "it" to happen.

Then a spark suddenly pulsed
through the muck and belched
an alien tune that I somehow knew was "it."
"It" was this thing called... LIFE!

It cracked the outer coating
of this sphere my messy insides
were pooled within, and when I spilled forth,
I was stunned to find that outside
of my previously protective shell,
I became something new, something whole,
but something different.

*This new version of me was astounded
at what my wondering eyes could see... EYES!
I actually had them now, and other senses
that allowed me to take in a whole new world!*

*I could inch along at my pace
and see things on my level and it
was an extraordinary experience!
I could see, feel, taste, hear, sense
this new world and it was such
a vast and marvelous creation,
that I knew... without a doubt:*

"This is LIFE!"

*And I lived it to the full,
on my level, at my pace,
and I was thrilled to be in the world...
and also of the world,
because the world still fed me.
I traveled around, on my level,
at my pace, until I was sure there
was no more for me to discover...
and I felt this pull to stand still
for a little while and rest.*

*Don't get me wrong, I was loving Life
and resistant to stop moving through it...
but I couldn't shake this internal,*

instinctive need to pause for just awhile.

*So, I gave the world a sleepy nod
with a promise to return soon,
and found a place to curl up...
just for a little while.*

*As I curled and quieted,
the strangest thing happened.
I began to feel wrapped, held, embraced, secure
...and I could hear these little whispers
from the outer walls:*

*"You are safe."
"You are loved."
"Rest in me..."*

*It was like the walls had
taken on a life of their own
and that life was calling... to... me.*

*Having been in the world,
these walls should've seemed restrictive
and confining, and yet somehow,
I had never felt so at peace.
The last thought I had before total stillness?...*

"So, THIS is life..."

*A shaking, a shuddering, a cracking
and my peaceful slumber was disrupted.
And I roused myself... well,
at least I thought it was myself.
But something was somehow... different.*

*I went to move and OUT burst
these strange parts of me that
I had never before seen!
They were wide and broad, bright and colorful,
and suddenly I found myself to
be extraordinary!*

*And they held **power**...
such power that I no longer crept
along the low places,
but soared among the highest heights!
I flew at my pace and at my level and oh,
the wonders and miracles I could see...
so much more than ever before.
And finally, I shouted:*

"THIS IS LIFE!"

*I learned quickly that this metamorphosis
did not come without hardship.
Though I could soar much higher,
I could also fall much farther.
And these beautiful, powerful wings*

*suddenly made me much more visible
and noticeable to those who would
seek to devour me. And with all their power,
these wings were often so delicate
that my faith in their ability to hold me
up would sometimes seem so fragile.*

*But when those doubtful times come,
I remember the voice in the stillness
that spoke to me with such love,
and its message keeps me aloft day by day:*

This is the way. This is the truth.

THIS is the life!

Toxic

Tread lightly, my friend...
for the life you know is at risk.
I wait quietly in the background as you travel
through your days and nights,
covered by a coat
of sensations and emotions
that are familiar and comfortable.
They are your go-tos, your autopilot,
the easy way to make it through.
Your lies, your complaints, your anger,
your frustration, your pain, yes -
they help you hold it down and keep it real,
but I...

I am toxic...

When I catch you unaware,
I seep into your bloodstream
and taint the source
of what's been driving you,
and my poison leaks from your pores,
polluting the air you've been breathing,
and infecting those closest to you.
I will take over your entire atmosphere
and make it mine and you will
become my carrier,
the key to my epidemic.

The perfect plague,
I'll make you highly contagious
to ensure that I'll be spread
to everyone you encounter, oh yes...

I AM toxic.

I challenge you to seek an antidote
that will destroy me,
because every time you think
you've lost me completely,
I assure you, I'm lurking just below the surface,
just waiting for the smallest spark
to reignite the fire I cause in your belly -
burning you from the inside out,
setting you ablaze with all that I am.

I am TOXIC.

And I dare you to catch me,
because I... am joy.
I am light, I am love, I am all that is good
and I am the toxic enemy
to the darkness that hopes to consume you.
I'm the smiling face on a bad day,
I'm the joyful song at the funeral,
I'm the laughter in the hospital room,
I'm the embrace after the fight,
I AM the ultimate biological weapon...

*if you would only use me
when you wage this war.*

*I'm more poisonous to darkness
than darkness is to me,
because even when I'm covered up or buried,
I continue to shine.
Darkness only exists <u>until</u> I arrive,
because once I do...
it breathes its last.
Because to the darkness,
I, the light;
I, the love;
I, the joy;*

I... am toxic.

I dare you to catch me, if you can...

Yeah, Write

They told me I was a poet -
an artist, with a gift.
And I laughed and said, "Yeah, right!"
Then the Voice whispered
in my soul and said, "Yeah... write."

Write because no one can make
the pen sing the way you do.
Sure, there have been others before
and will be more still to come, but you...
Yes, YOU... can transform ink into blood,
take plain paper and breathe into its fibers,
you can give LIFE!
To stories untold, secrets best kept,
sorrows held captive;
They lie dormant in
the vaulted hideaways
of these pages, a treasure
buried and waiting to be
unlocked by the next wayfaring stranger
unwittingly treading across the sand,
unaware that their footprints brought them
directly into your path... for a certain time...
which is now.

For who can nurture an idea
that hasn't been birthed?

*Aborted shortly after conception,
never to be nursed to the rhythm
of a beating heart; never nourished
and fed so that it would come to grow;
never cheered and championed
at its first successful step;
never molded and sculpted
with care and quality,
in expectation that its very presence
would mean something beautiful to the world.
Who will know? Unless... you write.*

*So, I say to you, "welcome, fellow poets!"
I'm so glad that you're here!
Glad that your footprints carried you
across the sands of time and space
so that today your journey might begin.
I speak for your children,
not those born of the body,
but created in the spirit that only YOU can
bring.
Because your words... yes, YOUR words...
can change lives, open doors, soothe hearts,
and awaken minds.
And every soul that you touch,
the offspring of your story, well...
they'll only make it here because of you.*

You'll look around this room,

*wondering who I'm speaking to,
and never believe that this message is for you.
But when the whisper enters your soul,
with a pen in its hand,
begging for your story to be told,
after you've laughed and said, "Yeah, right!"...
I say to you: Yeah...write.*

A Word on...
Maternal Sense

When I was in the process of choosing poems to include in the book, I decided on a somewhat broad theme of pieces about my general perspective on various topics. Whether I'm always successful or not in living it out, my life's central philosophy is rooted in one of my favorite phrases: "Do all things in love." So, I figured if I included my pieces that muse about life, perspective, and love, that should be sufficient. I did not plan to include any of my poems that were solely focused on specific people or circumstances in my personal life. But, I found one exception... a piece I wrote for my mother's birthday one year.

You might wonder why this piece was the exception to my rule not to include anything personal. It's simple. Because despite being written about a very special individual, this piece captures the essence of "doing all things in love" embodied in the form of my amazing mother. It is the unshakeable core of who she is and how she lives.

My understanding and certainty of what unconditional love looks like is rooted in my experience of life as a total immersion in her special brand of care. And so, my ode to her is indeed a necessary contribution to my written exploration and examination of love in all of its beautiful forms.

Maternal Sense

In my mother's eyes,
I've always been beautiful.
Brown baby, fat cheeks.
Gangly tween.
Pimply teen.
Freshman fifteen.
She beheld the wholeness of me.
Butterfly wings transposed
on my dissatisfied caterpillar body,
she saw me as perfection personified.
Not because I always got it right,
but because each misstep was growing me
into the one her eyes forever saw me to be.
The me through my mother's eyes.

To my mother's ears,
my every breath is a song.
Rhythmically composed to
the first audible beat of my heart,
it croons my life's melody,
gently underscored with her tones.
Interwoven in harmony,
where the chords resemble, but differ.
Never aiming to completely align,
and never seeking to part,
we glide on flowing rainbow chords;

A natural duet coloring the tune of life's chorus.
Sing of me, sing with me, sing through me,
my mother... music to our ears.

My mother tastes the flavor of my life.
She's sampled every morsel,
after adding just a sprinkle
of her own unique spices,
and my every action carries just a hint of her.
While she is a veritable feast
of the richest and most satisfying fare,
prepared with the most loving of hands,
I've still got work to do
and am stuck in the kitchen.
But she comes through the door,
draws me away from my culinary struggle,
and gently guides me to the table,
giving up her seat at the head just
to make me feel loved... and fed.
Taste and see the goodness of her love.

My mother's nose knows my every aroma,
and she follows the scent trail to my every need.
Whether near or far, she inhales
my fragrance and uncovers what lies beneath.
The acrid tang of my fear screams to her
and she offers the sweet breath
of courage and faith.

*The sharp bite of my pain drifts
across any distance and she dispels
its offensive odor with her
soothing, healing incense.
Together, we breathe in joy's perfume,
letting it seep into our skin,
while others catch a whiff as they pass by.
Her presence is my breath of fresh air.*

*A touch of my mother's hand gives only life.
Her reach extending far beyond family bounds,
infinite arms enfold and embrace the world.
I would clasp her hand in both of mine,
clutching it greedily for my own...
but to hold her to self is to dishonor her craft,
stifling the strokes of her nimble fingers,
as they long to weave and knit together
the strands of those in her care.*

*Come, rest your head upon her quilted heart
and feel your name, embroidered
and nestled there among the stitching.*

Speak

Speak... for your servant is listening.
Bending my ear, before ever feeling equipped
to walk whatever road I find myself next on.
Knowing that my own thoughts may seem solid,
but they should first be tested.
So, I set them ablaze, letting sage
Wisdom be the embers that incense the air.
Cleansing it of malformed philosophies
and dangerous ideas that might be shaped
by my every good intention...
but perhaps are not aligned
with the Divine Purpose of the moment.

I sit in stillness before the radiant fire
and only then... am I free to inhale,
deeply breathing in the vastness
of an omnipotent sky,
soaring alongside the filtered whispers,
gliding gracefully with the currents through
the previously clouded mind,
as dewdrops of Truth form
like pearls on my skin...
and then seep into my pores,
washing me from the inside
and pouring me out.

Listen... for your servant is speaking.

I stand here, filled to the brim.
A libation, offered to you and to Him,
because when I look at you, I must SEE Him,
or else my time in the wind was
for nothing other than catching a cool breeze
as I pass by, unchanged and unaffected.

<u>Your</u> every breath demands that I speak,
because every bone in my body
and every word from my pen was created
knowing that you and I would be here
in this place, at this time,
so that through this window
might pass a word that would
grant you wings... and take flight.

Believe, hope, dream, forgive, love.

On their shoulders, together can we fly.
But, I can only give what
I have first received.
So, I listen... and then... I speak.

Eulogize Me

I dream in loving memory of me.
Picturing my life through
the eyes of my future self.
Letting her fondly remember me
with the honor and pride that
I struggle to own in my present.
I'm fascinated by her willing guardianship
of my former hurts, gazing upon them
with smiling, joyful eyes.

In the present, I hold them
at arm's length, terrified that
by allowing them to merge with the triumphs,
I just might introduce
a poison that would taint
the goodness of the soul
I'm striving to grow.
Like her, I long to hold those
pains close to my heart and
rock them lovingly in my arms
until they fall gently into peaceful slumber,
having coalesced with their
more easily embraced counterparts
to form the whole.

What will they call her when her future ends?

Some would say, "joy bringer,"
for the way she sought to uncover
the most elusive of smiles,
buried under armored guards
of anger, distrust, hopelessness.

Others might say, "gifted one,"
remembering how she relentlessly
explored her own expression,
never resting until the messages
she promised to spread were set free.

A choice few would know her as "guardian,"
fiercely protective not only of her own,
but of all who suffer torment,
a defender of the fragile and wounded heart
that made such easy prey
for the world she knew.

I hope they would call her "dreamer,"
an answer to my prayer that one day
she would find herself loosed
from bonds of fear and doubt,
and step boldly onto her appointed path
into the unknown,
where Destiny divinely awaits her...
so that their work can begin.

But all will know her simply as "Love."

Because she strove to be His in every way,
the embodiment of His delight and affection,
seeing Him and <u>being</u> Him
every moment of every day.

I've seen her a few times, you know?...
this lady made in my image.
I caught a glimpse of her in the mirror once
and she looked deep into my eyes
with so much acceptance that
I knew it must be Her,
because it simply couldn't be me,
looking at me that way.
Even then, she cast no judgment,
but shared a smile full of secrets
that haven't yet been revealed.
I guess she knows some things that I don't.

*My husband... my husband says
I look just like her,
and it baffles me that he could
love both of us so completely.
I'm entranced by his devotion to her
and I can't wait to meet the woman
that has collaborated with me
to secure his heart.
She must be quite a sight to behold.*

*So, I dream in loving memory of <u>this</u> me,
looking forward to the day that I am
no more and, in becoming She that is to be,
finally... I'll rest in peace.*

"Yes, Lord!" Conclusion

A little over four years after it began, my journey of writing as an obedient vessel ended with the transition of my maternal grandfather. I was privileged to experience my first 37 years with all four of my grandparents as living and very much present in my life. The loss of the first of these four pillars was a blow that I didn't know how to face. The final piece I wrote in the "Yes, Lord!" journal was the tribute I read at my grandfather's funeral, entitled *Running*. In it, I discovered that my poetry was not intended solely for clever wordplay and creatively crafted storytelling for an audience's reflection and enjoyment. It was a haven, a safe place to unload and articulate my emotions on either end of the spectrum, and an instrument of healing.

Penning that piece on the final pages of the journal was symbolic and fitting on many levels, the most significant being a clear transformation in my writing. At the beginning of the journal, I self-deprecatingly referred to it as my "I'm supposedly a writer journal." Over those years, I came to understand that discovering myself as a writer was only the beginning. The final poem includes the declaration that I express through my pen because, "I know it holds the power to heal."

That statement would become the root, silently nurturing, spreading, and building the foundation of my budding and blossoming poet-tree (poetry) in the years to come. As I brought the book to a close, I claimed these truths:

> I Am a writer.
> I Am a healer.
> There is much work to be done.

PART TWO: "Soar"

*O*ver the course of the next few years, I found myself in the midst of unrelenting spiritual transformation. I obviously needed a new writing space and settled on a simple black journal, with a horizon-like scene etched in gold on the cover. The message on the front read, "In the midst of our lives, we must find the magic that makes our souls soar."

Following my grandfather's transition, I was truly in a state of wandering that turned out to be necessary preparation for facing the unknowns of life to come. At first, I did very little writing, except by request or for specific occasions. As is often the case, I look back and see just how many new and unexpected things were happening in my life. Moments of greatest joy and deepest pain that I carried and felt and allowed myself to experience, but did not articulate.

I understand now that it was this time in the Silence that set the stage for my true "finding". Somewhere in those moments, I caught whispers of my true Voice, saw glimpses of my most authentic Self, and began the work of setting her free to "soar". She saw herself in nature, allowed herself to speak her own truth amidst the cacophony of the world's constant clamor, and finally accepted the worth, value, and power of her uniquely crafted heart.

And so, she spoke...

Raindrop Song

I stood out in a light rain today.
Ignoring my umbrella and letting the cool drops
come to rest on me, unimpeded, undeterred.
And in their falling, a melody so sweet
crooned to my uncanopied heart.

Sweet words of affection,
appreciation... acceptance.
For me. Just as I am.
A lyrical declaration brushed across my soul
with the gentleness of a passing breeze...
and the power to transform my entire
understanding of the day ahead.

"Do you know..." they sang,
"...that each of us was created just for you?
That our journeys began far above this place,
but that our ultimate destination was only ever
going to be on your hand, your shoulder,
your eyelid? Can you see
that we were made for you?"

Each drop landed in its own place, no two drops
alike, and I alone was there to share
the experience with them.
Somehow, I was chosen, deemed worthy enough
to be the sole recipient of their attentions.

And I found myself... grateful.

*Sometimes the wind carried drops
to me that never would've arrived
without its push.
A few times, I imagined
that my tears might add a beautiful harmony
to the song as it played.
And I wondered if I would've listened
so openly had this been a storm instead.*

*I stood there... eyes closed, face raised...
and realized just how long it had been
since I listened with unplugged ears.
My precious devices weren't built for this...
I kept them tucked away in my bag,
dry and distant as they tend to be.*

*But I... I was made to hear raindrops,
singing across my skin,
calling me to listen with my heart,
and to dance in my soul.*

Wake Up

*Woke up this morning
and there's sunshine on my mind.
The kind that feels so good warming my skin.
Tingles like sparks of love walking all over me.
With an energy that knows
great moments await me this day.*

*That Light energy.
The essence of wisdom, joy, love,
fire, and understanding.
An expectation that newness will
make itself known to me,
as long as I keep my face turned
toward its rays, unsheltered.
No need for a block or a screen
that would limit its effect.
I am open and unabashedly naked,
letting it wash all over me.*

*While some may fear
the potential for burning,
I freely receive it and absorb it,
aware that any outer manifestation
of its impact is just an indication
that I've been changed from the inside out.
That the decision to bathe
in the Light is a surrender to its power.*

Realizing that to lie under its beam,
I must be willing to let it sear away
that which needs to die within me.
Knowing that my entire being
was created to regenerate, refresh, renew,
and revitalize itself afterwards.

So, I lie here, eyes closed, limbs outstretched,
heart and mind wide open to soak it all in.
When I arise and travel through my day,
I carry the light within me.

And I glow.

A Word on...
Meet Connie

When I began to travel somewhat off the beaten path of my original faith tradition, I learned a lot about the depth and breadth at its core. There are foundational beliefs and teachings there that resonate strongly with the deep truths and wisdom of other world religions and belief systems. It simply isn't talked about much unless you find yourself in circles and spaces with others who have ventured down those paths on their own journey. Once I gave myself permission to wander down hallways where the passage was a bit narrow, the light somewhat muted, I discovered an aspect of myself that had gone nameless for my entire life. That spark of wonder and joyful awe that rests just beneath my surface and is easily triggered by subtleties and seemingly insignificant events. The delighted curiosity that realizes the simultaneous enormity and "minisculity" of our world and our individual lives and thinks it's the coolest thing ever!

I am a contemplative.

There may be many definitions of that word, but I would personally describe a contemplative as someone whose understanding and appreciation of the Divine is grown and developed by "contemplating" life's moments and experiences with an awareness that there is always more happening than can be perceived or even imagined. When I learned the name of this part of my core self, it felt like my birth certificate had just received a subconscious upgrade! Finally, I could identify myself as one of many, understanding that there were others out there like me.

That sense of belonging was the solid ground I needed to feel secure in my intention to seek, to explore, and to educate myself about my own spiritual needs... and the courage to feed them.

Meet Connie

*Today is Easter Sunday
and also the last day of Passover.
I watched my usual virtual church,
then listened to a message from
a different kind of spiritual community.
I saw family and "almost" family.
I ate fast food and homemade food.
I played some and worked some.
I did some laughing and some crying.
I relaxed when I saw a bumblebee
and freaked when I saw a wasp.
I talked and I listened.
I gave and received a compliment.
I wished my daughter sweet dreams...
and received the same wish, with a kiss
from her sleepy toddler lips.*

*It was a full and fully beautiful day,
and here at the end, I feel Her presence.
A gentle knocking at my spirit's door,
asking for entry and some of my time.*

*"Hey Connie," I say, with a fond smile.
"I'm glad you're here and would love
to chat for a while."*

You see, Connie is me...
when I let my contemplative side run free.

She's the friend I can share the simplest
and sweetest moments of my day with,
without ever having to utter a word.
Spared from the need to attempt to explain
what a burst of joy truly feels like inside.
Never having to justify or articulate the tiny
pockets of simple but deep gratitude that cause
my eyes to well when no one is watching.
Knowing that She is fully aware every time
I just manage to overcome that catch
in my voice or that waver in my lip,
as I'm speaking something that moves me much
more deeply than my audience of the moment.
She understands every instant that my heart
becomes overwhelmed with emotion,
even when I sometimes don't get it myself.

Her very essence mirrors the soul
of the world and when She and I commune,
my soul rests in its native land,
at peace and at home.

You may not ever meet Connie.
She's my purest, gentlest,
most wide-open self
who speaks in a language

*that is foreign to this world.
And while she is rooted deeply enough
to boldly BE in every circumstance,
I've still got some catching up to do.*

*For now, I'll enjoy these quiet encounters
where we whisper of the melodies of the day...
and then sing our silent song,
as we soar among the stars.*

A Word on…
I, AManda

On January 20, 2021, Joe Biden was inaugurated as the 46th President of the United States. The country was gripped by so many signs of turmoil and disarray, that even an event which usually seems very stable and predictable was overshadowed by an underlying sense of anxiety about what might happen. I barely watched the broadcast, except to make sure that my daughters were there with my husband and I to watch the swearing in of Kamala Harris as the Vice President. Her position as the first woman and woman of color to hold this honor was indeed an important moment to witness and celebrate, and we enjoyed that brief portion of the event together before carrying on in our individual ways.

A short while afterwards, as I was preoccupied with my youngest daughter, my husband came and made me promise to go online later to, "watch the poet." Obviously very familiar with my love of spoken word, he didn't say much else, even though he was clearly overwhelmed by his own impression of the artist. Later that day, I heeded his advice and watched the country's first

National Youth Poet Laureate deliver her masterpiece, "The Hill We Climb." While I was in deed blown away by the poem, I had no idea that young Amanda Gorman would become such a major catalyst in my own journey.

To make a long and enjoyable story short, I wrote a poem that was inspired by Ms. Gorman's Inauguration Day performance, and I never would have guessed what came next. A co-worker heard my piece and loved it so much that she asked to share it with her two close friends, who she thought would appreciate it. One of those friends enjoyed the poem so much, that she asked me to be a guest on her new YouTube Channel. In her series, she would invite people engaged in various arts or other gifts to come have a conversation with her about whatever came up along the way.

During my "conversation," in addition to being able to share some of my poetry, it was literally the first time I spoke freely and openly about my spiritual journey. If I spent every page in this book, I would never be able to adequately describe the liberation, the joy, and the security I felt in that moment. I felt a rock-solid sense of rightness while we spoke and it shattered my willingness to settle for anything less than speaking my authentic truth. And it was that conviction, helped along by the insistence and enthusiasm of the host, that finally made this book a matter of necessity, rather than a nice idea.

Without any plans on my part, or awareness on hers, Amanda Gorman changed my life. I honor her contribution to the unveiling of my own highest and truest Voice with these words.

I, AManda

*"I AM ready," whispers the mirror with flesh
toned lips of a shade known by another name.*

*I AM adorned in simple jewels of tradition,
the words from my fingertips honoring
the sages and the ancestors,
as I speak for and speak over
my land, my people, my generation.*

*I AM crowned with wisdom that insistently
unites us, even as I offer muted
acknowledgment of that which divides us.*

*I AM robed with wings of beautiful birdsong,
soaring now freely toward a horizon
arrayed in hues that fill me with hope,
empower me with promise,
and awaken me with the light of a new day.*

I, AManda, am ready.

We must all be ready.

Move!

Time is officially up.
Time that I kept telling myself
was not enough, not sufficient,
not available, not allowed.
Time... a falsehood I've hidden behind
in my desperate, foolish attempts to stay safe.
Wrapped in a cocoon
of undeniably worthy obligation,
gleefully dodging the necessity
of an emergence that would not be denied.

For I... must... fly.

Time was the belief that my vocalized assent
was subdued by circumstances
that spoke in louder voices.
That speaking, singing, whispering
a heartfelt "Yes," in silent, humble tears
was not a blaring outburst
in the most sacred chamber,
rushing water, mighty wind,
unimpeded in their flow.
At last.

*Time is the shore I'm tempted to stand on,
the immovable preserver of the life I know...
I knew.*

*Time <u>was</u> the last thread holding
me tethered to its illusory safe harbor.*

*And as the waters part, revealing smooth
and inviting land, I know that it's time.*

I must go.

A Word on...
Move!

Yes, what began as a dream, a desire, a yearning to "soar" quickly brought the realization that in order to reach those alluring heights, I had to first be willing to fly. This would require something more pointed, purposed, and intentional from me: will and action. By nature, I am an easygoing, coasting sort of person, but I came to understand that for me to truly BECOME, I had to invest in my own unfolding. There is a place for letting go of the need to understand and control all of the intricacies of life. But for me, it was the call to act that I had not yet heeded.

As I began to spend more time listening to and connecting with the purest center of my very being, the Voice I had been nursing and cultivating over the years became less content with private musing and pondering, and more insistent about being heard. It was up to me to usher Her out of the Silence into sincerely spoken revelations about the world she perceived, the world she loved.

Intolerance 9-1-1

Emergency! Emergency!
It's urgent that I tell you immediately
that I... don't accept you.
I don't accept that action you took,
that decision you made, the way you look,
or whatever it was that brought you
to my otherwise divided attention.

Maybe you're new here,
but you see in my world,
we do things the way I say.
There's no room for me to have
to consider the possibility that I might not be
the center of your world.

After all, I am the source of the hive mind
that all of you need to be connected to,
so it's up to me to define how everything
and everyone in my world operates.
It's for your own good, you see?
But don't worry, I'll take good care of you.
All you have to do is follow my lead.
I have the secret weapon...
come closer and I'll tell you what it is.
It's my favorite word: "Should."
Can't you just feel it's power?

*Listen to me long enough,
watch me close enough,
and I'll use it to script your
entire existence for you.*

*I can tell you:
How you should think
Who you should trust
What you should wear
When you should act
Why you should make that decision…
But that's just the beginning!*

*For no additional cost,
I can just as easily tell you:
What you <u>shouldn't</u> believe
Where you shouldn't go
Who you shouldn't associate with
Why you shouldn't do what you were
JUST getting ready to do,
And why you shouldn't have done
what you just did.*

*By the time I'm through,
all will be right with the world,
Because you will live your life
and experience your days…
just as I say you should.
What could be greater?!*

Let me tell you, you don't want
to consider the alternative.
Where you exist in a space
that is uniquely your own.
Shaped, molded, and formed
by experiences that belong solely to you,
Driven not by the obvious superiority
of <u>my</u> thought process,
but left instead to think for yourself.
To make up your own mind
and to live from a place that is
dependent more on your own history
than what <u>I</u> say should be your core,
your foundation, your truth.
Why would you settle for
anything less than being just
like I say you should be?
Why would you do that to us?

If you won't be as I think you should...
then... then we'll have to live together
in this common space.
I'll have to step outside
of my own mind and peek into yours.
It would mean trying to understand
your existence when I'm
so deeply entrenched in my own.

*I'd have to realize that your decisions
and actions aren't sourced by my expectations.*

*When you invite me into your life,
I would have to enter as guest,
Learning my surroundings,
seeing them through unfamiliar eyes,
And accepting that your treasures
may differ from mine...
but they are no less precious.*

*When we cross paths, your destination
would have to be just as important as mine...
And your safe arrival just as necessary.*

*When you shed tears, I would have
to consider that if I can't cry with you,
it doesn't mean you have no reason to weep.*

*When we disagree, maybe... just maybe...
each of us has the right to be right.
And maybe... just maybe...
we might try to be...
Maybe we could learn to be...
If we worked together, maybe... just maybe...
We would become intolerant
of our own intolerance.*

Tell My Daughter

Tell my daughter that she's beautiful.
Not so that she'll face herself in the mirror
and work to hide every flaw.
Not even to make her believe that inner beauty
is more valuable than appearance.
No... tell her that she EXISTS...
and <u>that's</u> the beautiful thing.

That from the creative spark
of her conception
to the self-directed journey
to her current state,
she is a masterpiece
so carefully and elaborately crafted.

She, simultaneously the muse and the canvas;
the paint and the brush that wields it;
the artwork and the craftswoman
that brings it to life... such a creature
of wonder and worth!
Beautiful in brokenness and pain,
and in peace and joy.

Beauty is in the eye of the beholder,
because to behold her is
to see the beautiful truth
of her very beingness... no mirrors required.

So, TELL HER... and don't ever let her forget.

Tell my daughter that she's powerful.
Don't spin her tales of fragility,
when you know damn well
the blows she'll take, survive,
and overcome every day of her life.
Implore her to give herself extra credit
for her daily tries and triumphs,
because every other scorecard
will chalk it up as "woman's work."
Point value: Zero.

Resist the temptation to label
her weaker, because of YOUR need to protect,
provide, dominate, and direct.
And don't you ever criticize
or make your own self-absorbed demands
of her body, when that powerhouse can support,
sustain, and bring forth
a whole 'nother being... or several at once!

Even should she have no plans
to do so (because yes, that's a thing),
the very potential is a force to be reckoned with.

How dare you attempt to coerce her
into dependence, suggesting
that she NEEDS someone else

to make her whole?
Or that her primary role
and responsibility is to
support and sustain others,
to be the wind beneath their wings,
while hers lay wilted and withered
from neglect, not a single whisper left
to cause even the tiniest flutter.
No, you TELL HER of her strength...
and don't ever let her forget.

Tell my daughter that she's worthy.
Not because she needs your validation...
there you go trying to tether her
to your ego's demands again.
No, you tell her because you owe it
to the Universe to honor her treasured soul.
You owe it to God to honor His creation.
Is it really so costly to use your words
to affirm her rather than
degrade or demean her?

Seems to me you're getting a sweet deal.
Because in truth, she's more than worthy
of your time, your attention,
your respect, and your love.

*But she's much more likely
to give all of hers away
because she appraises YOUR worth
as immeasurable in comparison to her own.
So, you tell her...
Hell, tell EVERYONE...*

*Acknowledge her beauty.
Accept her power.
Appreciate her worth...
And don't YOU ever forget.*

Color Blind

You make me see red.
Be it your state of mind
or your state of residence,
it bleeds across my sight
to color my every vision of you
with unrelenting rage.

And you, you make me so blue.
Weighing me down
with your burdened cynicism,
demanding that I cast off hope and faith
in favor of skepticism and doubt.

You, I find covered in green.
Infected by your ravenous hunger
to gain and possess.
And you dare to claim independence,
when your addiction is fully funded
at another's expense.

Your vision of black is dark and menacing.
An unknown that you fear
because you can't see past its hue.

Your white is cold and unfeeling.
So assured of its purity and superiority,
that it can't possibly find common ground
with its tinted peers.

Hatred.
Judgment.
Condemnation.
Fear.
Distrust.

These are the windows
that shade our encounters,
blinding us to the truth.
Color is, after all, just an illusion…
a trick of the mind's eye,
attempting to process light.

But the light, at its source, is the same.

United.
Whole.
One.

Dare to see.

A Word on...
And Love Held the World

May 25, 2020 is a day that many people around the world will never forget. It was Memorial Day here in the US, but certain to be unlike any other, since the world was gripped in the terrifying clutches of a global pandemic.

It was also the day my maternal grandmother peacefully made her transition from this life. After so many years of living with dementia, thankfully in the best possible care the family could ever have hoped for, it was clear that she was readying to journey on.

I remember feeling uncertain of what to do, once we knew the time was drawing near. I remember awkwardly calling her caregiver and asking her to hold the phone by the bedside so she could hear me and my daughters tell her we loved her and that everything was okay. I remember wondering if what I said was right or enough or appropriate. But most of all, I remember being grateful that I made the call anyway, sparing myself from the possibility of feeling regret for not taking that precious opportunity while I still had the chance.

Obviously, the people of the world wouldn't remember that day because of mourning my grandmother. No, while I was facing the personal loss, the world was in an uproar over the killing of George Floyd by a Minneapolis police officer, the whole tragic experience captured on video and spreading across the globe as rampantly as the COVID-19 virus.

George Floyd's death represented a sort of global tipping point for so many issues and challenges, and the response and reaction were swift and intense. Anger, rage, pain, outrage, despair, hopelessness, fear, hatred, blame; there was seemingly no limit to the spectrum of emotions sparked by that day.

At the same time, some very clear and unapologetic lines began to be drawn in the proverbial sand on TV, social media, in family and friend relationships, in the workplace, between corporations and consumers, and everywhere people could be found. What used to seem like common ground suddenly became very rocky, and people became more wary and skeptical about whether they felt they could trust their footing in certain settings.

I emerged from the cloud of grief over my

grandmother into this burning, violent haze over the world I knew, and it was difficult for me to function. While so many of my friends and loved ones were seething and overcome with anger, I remained in a state of grief. No longer fixated on the life of my grandmother, but instead for the very soul of the world. I later recounted that I felt like I was embodying the heart of Mother Earth, experiencing deep sadness because of a nearly audible ripping apart of the fabric of life housed here.

At the same time, I recognized that mine was not a commonly held response to the issues of the day. I wasn't angry, I didn't boil over with the outcry for justice, I hadn't suddenly shifted into a new worldview. I was just sad about the state of the world that made way for such a time. But I felt clearly that my perspective would not be welcome in such a climate, so I stifled my voice, shut down my feelings, and walked around in a bit of a fog... until I had a revelation.

This was not the type of silence that fuels and feeds me. It was instead a muting of the authentic Voice that I had developed and my spirit was no longer willing to tolerate such blatant dishonor and disregard of her need to speak... and be heard.

For the first time in my life, I saw clearly that I was going to pen something that I <u>knew</u>, without a doubt, was to be shared broadly. I didn't know when or how... hell, it hadn't even been written yet... but it was cemented in my very being that it must go forth.

And so, it shall...

And Love Held the World

In the twinkling twilight,
the child stood still
with troubled and turbulent eyes.
"I'll tell you a story," said a voice on the wind.
"It's as timeless as the skies."

"It begins the day I met you,
and it's my favorite tale.
It travels 'cross all space and time,
and ends when we prevail.

It tells of your great promise
since the day you came to be,
and all the ways you've lived up
to the dream you are to me.

I'll show you what a mighty work
began when you were born,
and share how much we triumph
when you pass through each new storm.

It covers ground that's rocky
when you thought you'd lost your way,
and shows that when together,
you and I can face each day.

So, pause and rest and listen,
just a moment... maybe two.
And I'll show you my favorite gift:
the precious Truth of you.

I know the things that haunt you,
whether hidden or in plain sight.
But I will always cover
and protect you with my light.

I've heard your cries of mourning
and your silent screams of rage.
And I've overseen your healing,
carried through from age to age.

I've seen your wars and fighting,
even as you long for peace.
And yet, I've known the best of you...
my faith in you won't cease.

When you choose to disregard me,
it's your distance that I grieve.
But you've never been without me,
no matter what you may believe.

You've read and written stories,
trying to evaluate your worth.
To me, you're simply priceless...
and have been so since your birth.

I only see you beautiful,
not your actions or your kind,
and when you doubt your goodness,
there's no question in <u>my</u> mind."

"Who are you…?" said the wondering child,
"…for you must have a name."
"Call me anything you like.
I'll still remain the same.

My child, it's time for you to rest,
a moment to be still.
I have the answers that you seek.
I'll share them, if you will.

You see, I long to carry you
to places far and near.
There's power when you speak for me
to those who need to hear.

Draw near to me, come very close,
and I'll show you my way.
Just tune your ear to seek my voice,
to guide the words you say."

"Yes, come to me," the voice implored,
with hand gently unfurled.
The child stepped forth into its palm…
and Love held the World.

A Word on...
Numb

After nearly a year of highly charged emotions, coupled with difficult but necessary conversations, the world watched the trial of George Floyd's killer closely and with bated breath. There was a huge sense that this particular verdict would not only declare the fate of the officer, but of the entire nation.

When the guilty verdict was announced, there was such relief and jubilation among the people, including full-on celebrations and parties. Overwhelming cheers and joy in the name of justice being done, and it truly was like that first huge exhale after holding your breath for too long. For many people, it was an emotional release and, I think, a real sense of thankfulness that at least this went in a direction that shouldn't cause another immediate explosion of protests and demonstrations among the masses.

And once again, I found myself in uncommon territory. While I was relieved that the trial had ended in a way that should at least not cause a new uproar, I still watched the face of the officer when the verdict was read. I didn't really try to examine him or analyze his expression. I just saw him as a fellow human being whose actions and choices had left an indelible mark on the world and on anyone who was closely associated with him. I saw someone whose future had been stripped away by whatever elements of his past allowed him to become the person he was now.

I didn't really feel inclined to celebrate a win... for me, it was just a loss of a different kind.

Having a better understanding of my own needs in moments like this, I turned to my pen for solace.

Numb

*Some might say it's strange
for an empath to go numb.
When one's very existence is tuned
to the finest sliver of emotion,
it would seem that it should
be nearly euphoric to be amidst such intense
relief, hope, satisfaction, joy, and optimism.
Having wept with the world and its people,
why not now rejoice
in this moment called "justice"?
Where so many have found, discovered,
realized, or accepted their worth anew,
having forfeited it to those they never trusted
to secure it... then raging at their bankruptcy.*

*This incredible release,
a deep sigh from the streets,
should feel like a breeze through the soul,
a collective cleansing,
readying the way forward.*

And I sit... numb.

*It's a buffer zone, you see.
Because empathy does not sequester
itself to only hear the arguments*

for the side of "good."
It is the most balanced of Libra's scales,
equal parts objective party
and innocent bystander,
trapped by the in-between that MUST
acknowledge that there are no actual sides,
only a fractured, fragmented whole
that has no sense of its true self.

It is the soul of Pangaea, Gaia,
ripped apart by schizophrenia,
calling it humanity
and daring to declare itself superior
to other forms of harmonious being.

An empath is that center, embodied
and stretched to its farthest limits,
desperately clinging to each precious star
in its vast galaxy,
no matter how far, how lost,
or how close to its own destruction,
enfolding that single flicker
in an embrace that says,
"You are still one of mine."

The Bible says to weep with those who weep,
and rejoice with those who rejoice,
but neglects guidance for the empath's call
to stand in the center and do both at once.

*So, don't mind me if I don't partake
of your bounteous overflow of emotion today,
no matter what "side" you're on.*

*I'm sparing myself from my own
relentless compassion and going numb.*

A Word on...
The Creed

The greatest gift I have received over these past few years is an understanding of the necessity and the power of knowing and speaking MY Truth. Having spent much of my life being trained, taught, and encouraged to believe certain things, the path to becoming a seeker of Truth was a difficult one for me. My nature as a rule follower made it particularly challenging to grant myself permission to explore out-of-bounds. I believed that I would not find validation or approval from most of my closest spiritual companions... whether that was true or not is a different matter.

In any case, that realization was hard to face, as I do not really consider myself to be a solitary person or a rebel of any kind. That being said, while I had doubts about the suitability of my existing support network, I was crystal clear that I could not progress without one. I often work through my own thoughts best by letting them out in a safe space for musing, and while my writing was a significant help, I desired a guide through this unfamiliar territory.

In my seeking, I encountered several spiritual

directors whom I worked with only briefly, but each helped me find an essential piece of the new spiritual foundation I was building. It was one of these gifted vessels that encouraged me to stop wrestling with, and analyzing, my previous statements of belief (as handed to me by my original faith tradition) and to instead write my own. A declaration of my own making that may be subject to change over time, but was no less true for it in the present. "Write your own creed," the wise counselor suggested, providing me with both the permission and the freedom to speak MY Truth in my way.

I offer it now to you, as a culmination of the work and the works that have come before, with gratitude to you for traveling with me this far, and with hope that it will contribute to your own beautiful unfolding.

The Creed

I wanna talk about God.
The God I know, not the one
that was introduced to me so long ago,
masqueraded by every well-intentioned
attempt to help us get better acquainted.
No, this God comes to me bared
and unrestrained,
unable to do any less than overwhelm me
with love and acceptance.
Constantly whispering words declaring
my worth, my capability, my perfection,
my undeniable goodness as one of its own.

God the Father,
God the Mother,
God the beautiful union
of each dichotomous idea,
the resulting perfection ringing with soaring,
swelling harmonies that move me
to tears each time I'm still enough
to hear them in my soul.
This is the God I know.

I wanna talk about Christ.
The Christ that Jesus discovered
and demonstrated,

but didn't imagine that we would
never claim as our own.
The very tangible, individualized core self
that remains constantly in tune with God,
even when I forget to consciously connect.
Unfazed by my beliefs and unimpeded
by any religious prescriptions or precepts,
my Christ remembers me undiminished,
unharmed, untainted, and unaffected,
and is constantly ready
to remind me of that Truth.

This Christ is my tether to all of Creation,
and vibrates with the necessary energies
to draw me closer to that which supports
and furthers my soul's purpose
in this lifetime… and all others.
Christ in me, in you, in all is
the purest center of peace
that rests undisturbed
by any and all other ideas.
It is simply the part of me
that KNOWS it is one with God
and never forgets.
This is the Christ I know.

I wanna talk about the Spirit.
The wind, the whispers,

the constant companion that holds my hand
and leads me back to Christ's shore,
when I have drifted.
This is God's beacon, the lighthouse,
the signpost, and the breadcrumbs.
But also God's voice, translator,
messenger, and agent.
Spirit escorts God to wherever
and whenever I happen to be,
sometimes even when I haven't
been looking for it.
And when I do actively
and intentionally go seeking,
Spirit eagerly and enthusiastically
guides me to the door,
excited and anticipating the unspeakable
joy we will find once we enter.
This is the Spirit I know.

This indescribable existence I know as God
is best understood as love in every form.

God loves me in falling raindrops,
falling snow, and falling leaves;
Loves me with the scent
of wildflowers and in birdsong;
Loves me even through the spider crawling
on my window and the mosquito's bite,
though it may be harder for me to see it that way!

God loves me with my youngest daughter's smile
and my oldest daughter's laughter,
and even through my stepdaughter's
rejection and distrust.

God loves me with the breaths
my two angels never took,
and the tears we have all cried in their memory.

God loves me with my father's mother's care
and with my mother's mother's memories;
with my father's father's bruised pride
and my mother's father's unwillingness
to submit.

God loves me with my husband's
every single breath and every moment
we spend together or apart.

And God has loved me every day
since I took breath in this life,
with the acceptance, pride, understanding,
and support of my mother, father, and brother.
And on and on and on...

God loves me with the laughter
and joy I share with others,
be they stranger or friend;
Loves me in each shared moment

and experience in a way that is uniquely mine
to understand and appreciate.

God loves me by allowing me
to be love to others
in ways that are natural to me…
and by flooding me with humble joy
at each encounter.

God loves me by drawing me step by step,
moment by moment, towards that
which is mine to do.

But most of all, God loves me because I AM.
And there is no further requirement
or stipulation beyond that.

This I believe.
This I know.
This I declare.

Amen.

"Soar"
Conclusion

At the start of 2021, I participated in my still somewhat new annual tradition of a White Stone Ceremony, which is a practice I discovered through the Unity church. To simplify down to its most basic explanation, it is a ceremony through which one spends time connecting with the inner core and most authentic Self to find a word, phrase, or idea to serve as a primary year-long theme which is then written on a white stone and kept close as a reminder throughout the year. For the first time in my experience, the facilitator of the ceremony noted the possibility that an image might come through rather than a word. In my case, it was both.

On my rock, I sketched a crude drawing of a sunny horizon, with a few birds in the sky; the word that came to me was "soar." It was a few days later before I realized that the image I drew was eerily similar to the cover of my journal (in my years of less writing, I hadn't paid much attention to the front of the book) and that the message specifically referenced the desire to "soar." Needless to say, I found great peace and joy in this affirmation of what my soul had been calling for, and gratitude that I had finally dedicated myself to listening and acting on Her behalf.

At last, I hear Her... and now, so have you.

EPILOGUE

My oldest daughter and I love to watch the sky and capture beautiful images of the ever changing, but always fascinating sky. Its clouds have mastered the art of portraying infinite and boundless possibilities, while resting in complete silence. On a seemingly regular day, sitting in a normal stretch of rush hour traffic on a typical drive home from work, I glanced at the sky and came face-to-face with my own infinite, boundless self. As I sat transfixed, she revealed Herself to me, with complete clarity and definition.

In my willingness to heed the call to expand outside of previously perceived boundaries, and my enthusiastic and heartfelt desire to look beyond my well-known horizons, I find myself following that cloud-like wisdom more frequently. As you have traveled through these pages, whatever images or impressions you have gained of me may certainly carry some measure of truth. Along the way, I can only hope that you have found something in this journey that has made your time spent worthwhile.

Whatever the case may be, with gratitude I leave you with this final piece... the essence and declaration of who I now KNOW myself to be.

Namaste.

Cloudy Wonder

I saw my True Self in the sky, today.
She was resting in the clearest cloud
I've ever seen, and I've never gazed upon
a more beautiful sight.

The first thing she showed me was her reach,
outstretched in a gesture
of simultaneous receiving and giving;
Her open hand completely at rest,
content to hold its position
in the space between holding on and letting go.

And she knelt there.
Secure in her surrender
to the space created just for her.
Neither supplicant nor subservient,
there was power in her lowering,
fueled by her desire to connect
with the earthen soul,
she nestled among root and soil
and water and sky.
In each, she found home.

She had wings!
They weren't big and extravagant,
but small and close to her body.

I had no doubt of their strength for flight,
but became enamored of their subtlety.
In her, I found my affirmation
that there is just as much work
to be done in the small and simple,
as in the large and lofty.
Both necessary, worthy, and beautiful.

Her hair, an Angela Davis-worthy 'fro,
unapologetically crowning
the seat of her consciousness,
awareness, and intellect.
She showed no interest in adorning herself
in a particular manner deemed acceptable.
I saw no willingness to align
with any static or immovable principle.
Just a security independent
of expectation or demand.
She was content to simply be...
and just as content to become.

But the largest Truth she showed me
was the strength of her heart.
A solid stream burst forth,
an explosion of her essence projected
directly into the vastness of her surroundings.
It both comingled with other
like-fashioned auras...
and delved fearlessly

into darker, dissimilar masses.
The sky around her was peppered
with varying shades, but in each one,
she saw glimpses of herself.
And so she relentlessly expressed
from her depths an inexhaustible
and incomparable force: Love.

She turned her head my way
with a playful tilt and an affectionate glance.
"I see you," she said.
"Now, it's your turn. See me... and see you."

"Cloud E Wonder"
by Jackie W.

This image was drawn to mirror the photograph I took that inspired the "Cloudy Wonder" piece. It carries the alternate name of the poem, referring to this "Cloud" version of "E Wonder," a nickname given to me by my husband.

ABOUT THE AUTHOR

*E*rin Wiley, the person, could be reasonably described in terms of who she has been throughout her life. She is deeply rooted and supported by the love of family as a devoted daughter, sister, wife, mother, and friend. A trained and experienced statistician and fan of puzzles and mysteries since childhood, she is a thinker - quick to assess and analyze in an effort to solve and resolve every situation. She has found success over the years as a student, dancer, track and field athlete, and singer. This is who Erin Wiley has been.

As a writer, Erin Wiley is an instrument of the Soul voice that is ever longing to speak and be heard. She is an unfolding spiritual manuscript, constantly being written and rewritten as a work of Divine Love. With genuine affection for wordcraft, she writes from the space between, always seeking to offer perspective, foster unity, and promote peace within. With each

performance or written piece, she invites her audience into a space of warmth, acceptance and unconditional love. She has the heart of a healer and considers her life as an opportunity to build the Beloved Community, each and every day. This is who Erin Wiley is becoming.

Knowing who she has been and discovering who she is becoming is an ongoing journey that reveals itself best with pen in hand. This is what she has learned and understands, this is what she accepts and honors as her calling… this is why Erin Wiley Writes.

Connect with Erin!

Website: erinwileywrites.com
Email: erinwileywrites@gmail.com
Like **Erin Wiley Writes** on Facebook!

www.ingramcontent.com/pod-product-compliance
Lightning Source LLC
LaVergne TN
LVHW020438070526
838199LV00063B/4780